T0198410

The Freeze Dance Book

Written by:

Alyssa Wilburn

Illustrated by:

Tabitha Hamm

To order additional copies of this book, contact:
Xlibris
844-714-8691
www.Xlibris.com
Orders@Xlibris.com

ISBN: Softcover   978-1-6641-6018-7
       EBook   978-1-6641-6017-0

Print information available on the last page

Rev. date: 02/24/2021

The Freeze Dance Book

Let's play the freeze dance game! Everybody get ready. Stretch your arms up and then to the side. Wiggle your hips from side to side. Get ready to dance!

Dance, Dance. Dancing, dancing and move around. Dance your body to the left. Dance your body to the right. Turn around and touch the ground. Dance, dance, Dance! Stop when I say...

FREEZE!

Get ready to skip

Stretch your arms up and then to the side. Wiggle your hips from side to side.

Skip, skip. Skipping, skipping, move around. Skip your body to the left. Skip your body to the right. Turn around and touch the ground. Skip, skip, skip! Stop when I say...

FREEZE!

Get ready to waddle

Stretch your arms up and then to the side. Wiggle your hips from side to side.

Waddle, Waddle. Waddling, waddling, move around. Waddle your body to the left. Waddle your body to the right. Turn around and touch the ground. Waddle, waddle, waddle! Stop when I say...

FREEZE!

Get ready to jump

Stretch your arms up and then to the side. Wiggle your hips from side to side.

Jump, Jump. Jumping, jumping, move around. Jump your body to the left. Jump your body to the right. Turn around and touch the ground. Jump, jump, jump! Stop when I say...

Ready to play again?

Printed in the United States
By Bookmasters